Amazing Archaeology

Terracotta Army

by Julie Murray

Dash!
LEVELED READERS
An Imprint of Abdo Zoom • abdobooks.com

Level 1 – Beginning
Short and simple sentences with familiar words or patterns for children who are beginning to understand how letters and sounds go together.

Level 2 – Emerging
Longer words and sentences with more complex language patterns for readers who are practicing common words and letter sounds.

Level 3 – Transitional
More developed language and vocabulary for readers who are becoming more independent.

abdobooks.com

Published by Abdo Zoom, a division of ABDO, PO Box 398166, Minneapolis, Minnesota 55439.
Copyright © 2022 by Abdo Consulting Group, Inc. International copyrights reserved in all countries.
No part of this book may be reproduced in any form without written permission from the publisher.
Dash!™ is a trademark and logo of Abdo Zoom.

Printed in the United States of America, North Mankato, Minnesota.
102021
012022

Photo Credits: Alamy, Getty Images, iStock, Shutterstock
Production Contributors: Kenny Abdo, Jennie Forsberg, Grace Hansen, John Hansen
Design Contributors: Candice Keimig, Neil Klinepier

Library of Congress Control Number: 2021940201

Publisher's Cataloging in Publication Data

Names: Murray, Julie, author.
Title: Terracotta Army / by Julie Murray
Description: Minneapolis, Minnesota : Abdo Zoom, 2022 | Series: Amazing archaeology | Includes online resources and index.
Identifiers: ISBN 9781098226695 (lib. bdg.) | ISBN 9781644946428 (pbk.) | ISBN 9781098227531 (ebook) | ISBN 9781098227951 (Read-to-Me ebook)
Subjects: LCSH: Terra-cotta sculpture, Chinese--Qin-Han dynasties, 221 B.C.-220 A.D--Juvenile literature. | China--Antiquities--Juvenile literature. | Excavations (Archaeology)--China--Shaanxi Sheng--Juvenile literature. | Funerary decorations--Juvenile literature. | Excavations (Archaeology)-Juvenile literature. | Archaeology and history--Juvenile literature.
Classification: DDC 931.04--dc23

Table of Contents

Terracotta
Army
4

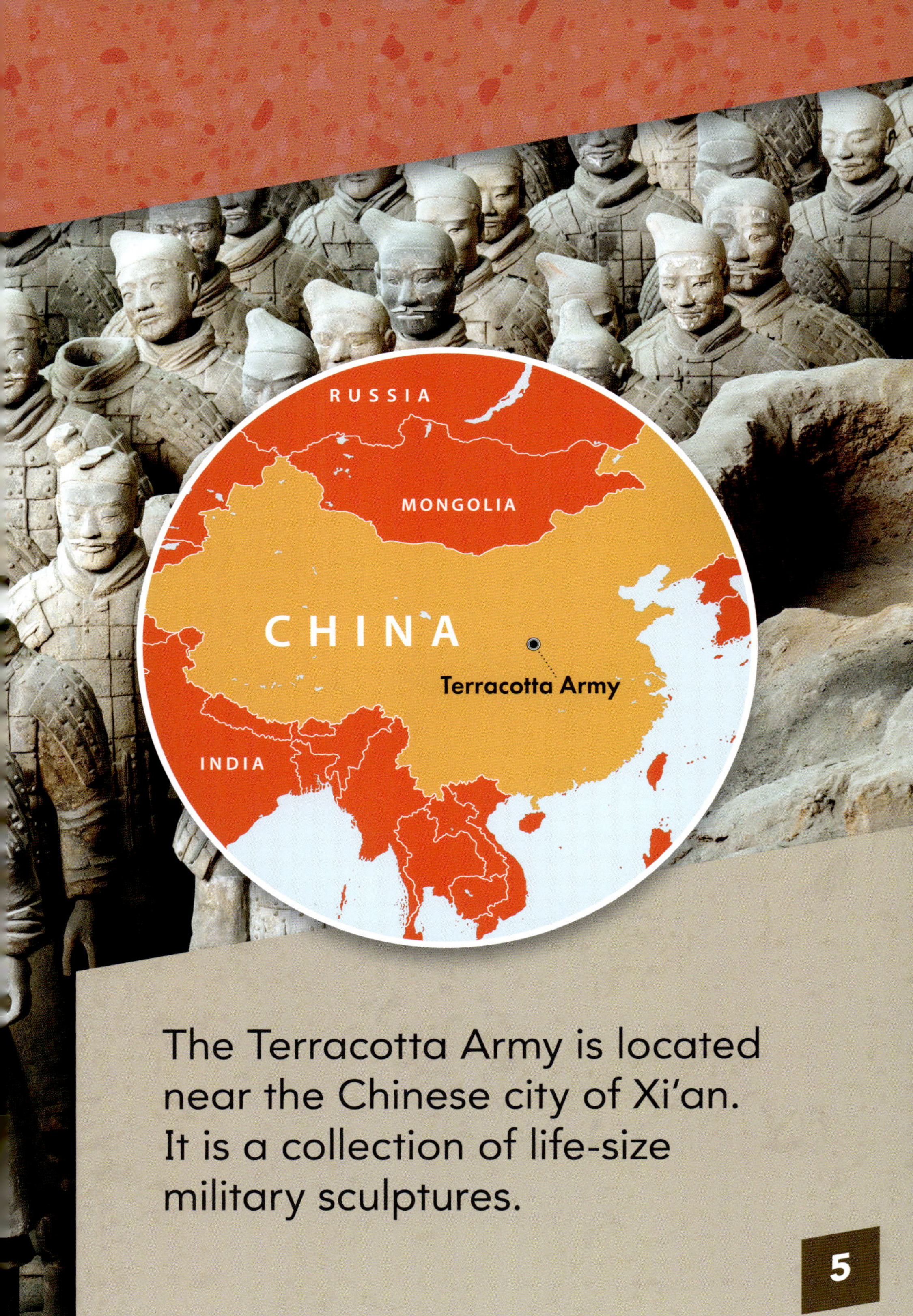

The Terracotta Army is located near the Chinese city of Xi'an. It is a collection of life-size military sculptures.

The **terracotta** sculptures are more than 2,250 years old! They date back to the Qin **dynasty** in China.

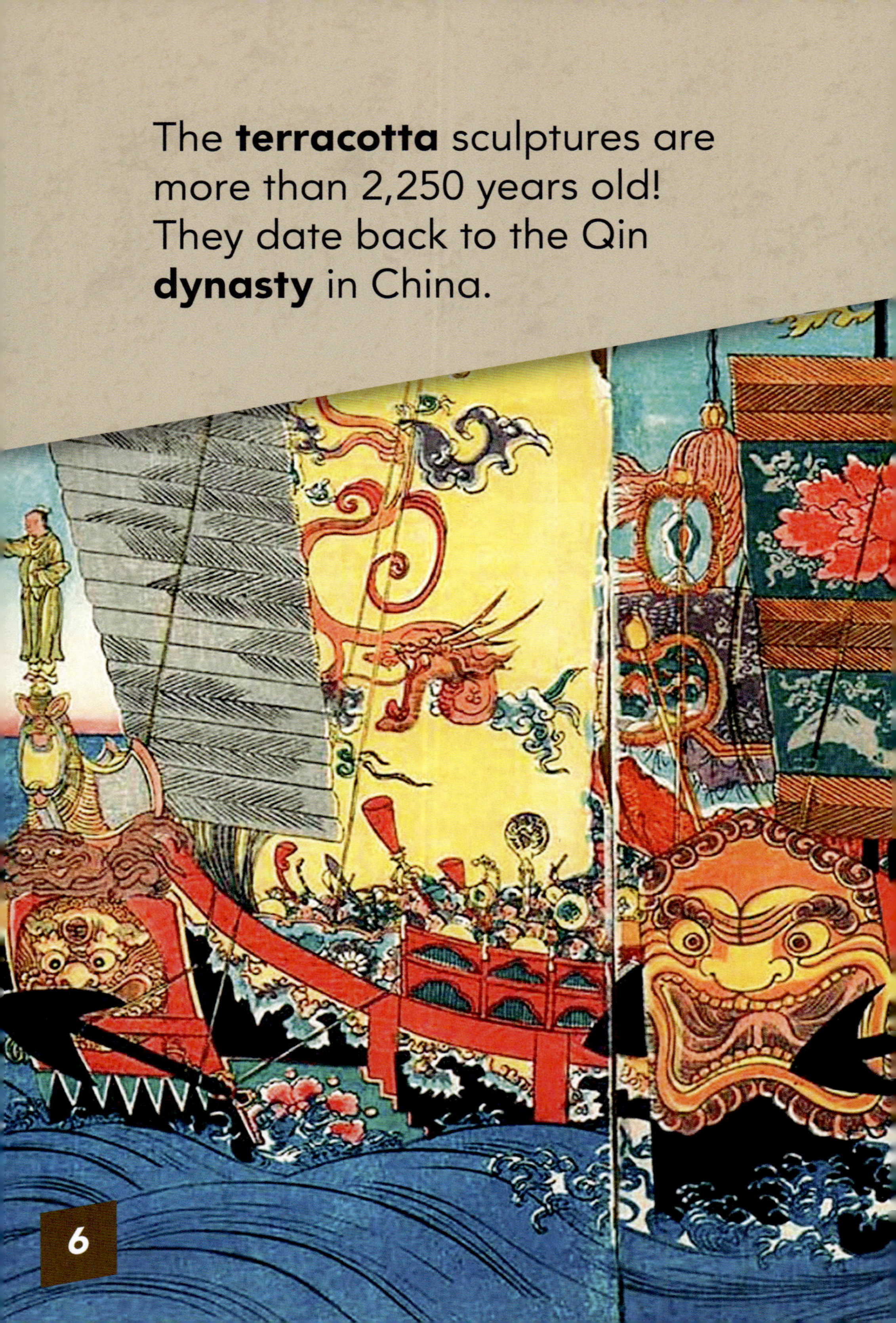

CHINA'S FIRST EMPEROR
AND THE
TERRACOTTA WARRIORS

Qin Shi Huang was the first **Emperor** of China. He had the Terracotta Army built to protect him in the afterlife.

Construction began soon after Qin Shi Huang took power. He ruled until his death in 210 BCE. His burial site is near the Terracotta Army.

11

Discovery

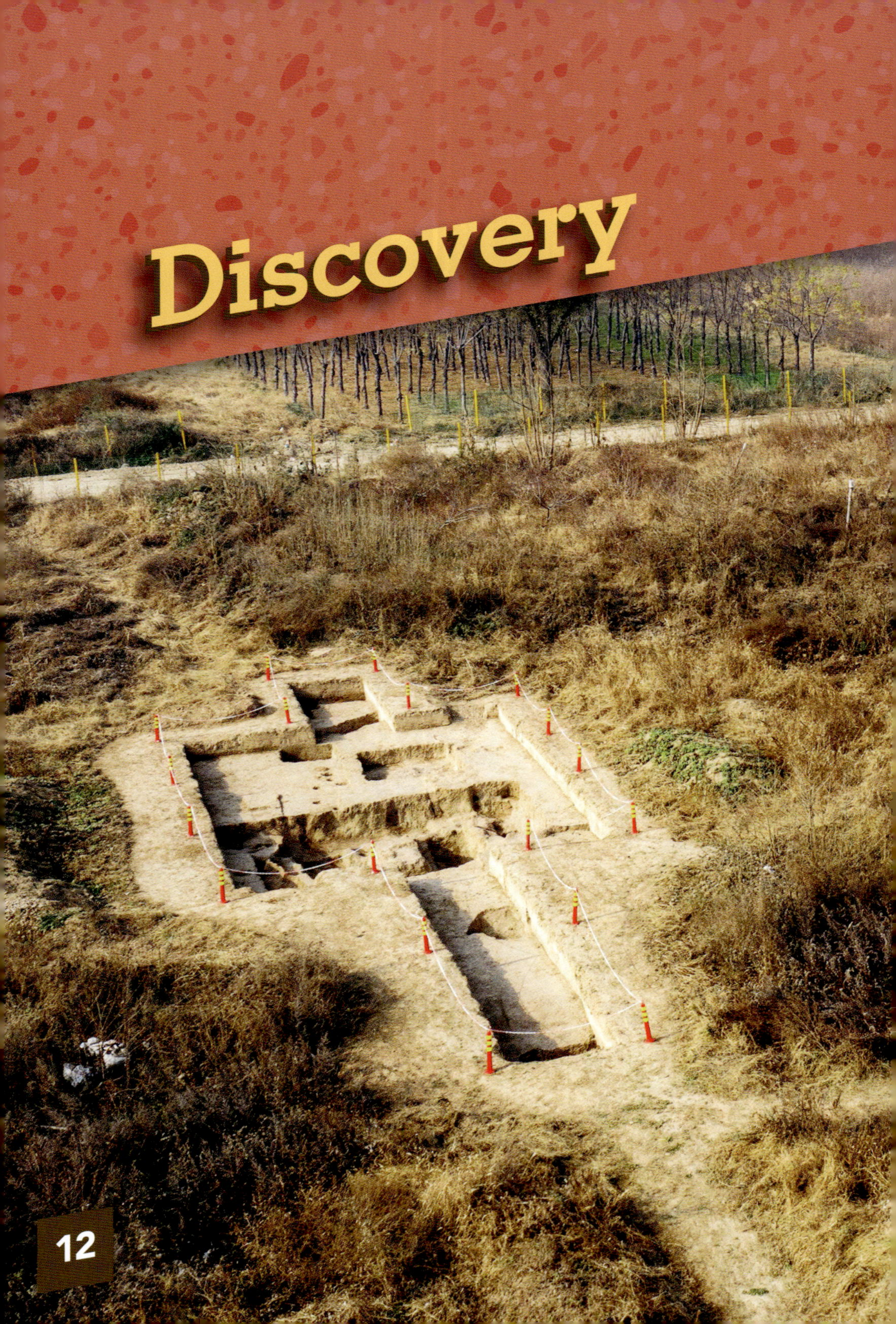

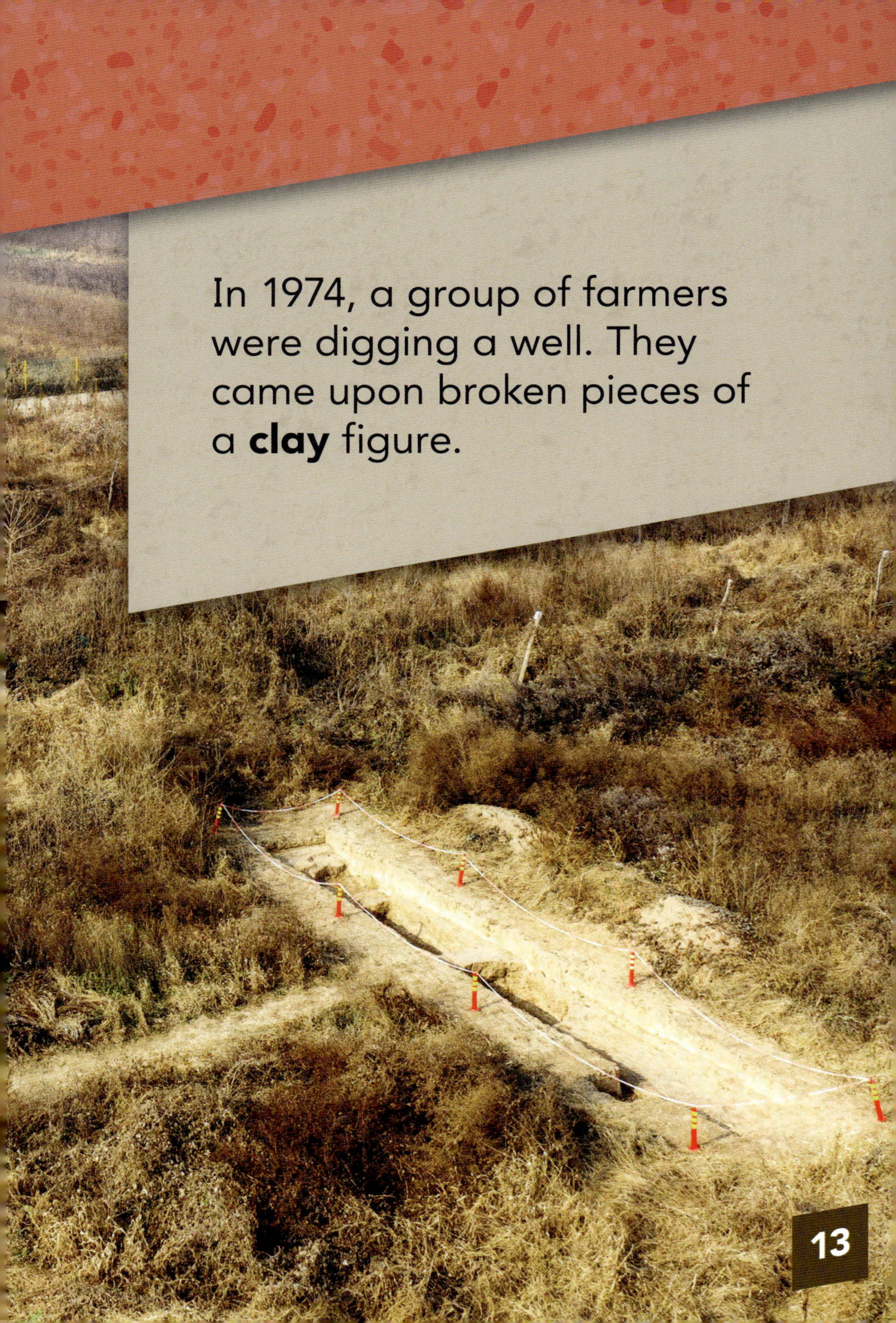

In 1974, a group of farmers were digging a well. They came upon broken pieces of a **clay** figure.

Excavators have since discovered three different pits. The pits contain thousands of sculptures of warriors and horses.

The warriors stand nearly 6 feet (2m) tall. They are in line formation, ready for battle!

The warriors are in full armor.
Each one also has different
facial features, hair, and
clothing. No two are alike.

18

Today

Today, the Terracotta Army is on display at a museum that was built at the site. Information about Qin Shi Huang and the Qin **dynasty** can also be found at the museum.

- The Terracotta Army is a World Heritage Site. It sits on about 16 acres of land (6.5 ha).

- More than 700,000 workers helped sculpt the Terracotta Army.

- The warriors once held real weapons. Some remains of weapons have been found. But most were **looted** or have rotted away.

Glossary

clay – moist, stiff earth that is used for making brick, pottery, and tile.

dynasty – a series of rulers from the same family or group.

emperor – a ruler of an empire.

looted – taken by force.

terracotta – (also terra-cotta) a glazed or unglazed fired clay used especially for the making of sculptures and pottery, and in architecture.
Terra cotta is Italian (from the Latin *terra cocta*) for "baked earth."

Index

Online Resources

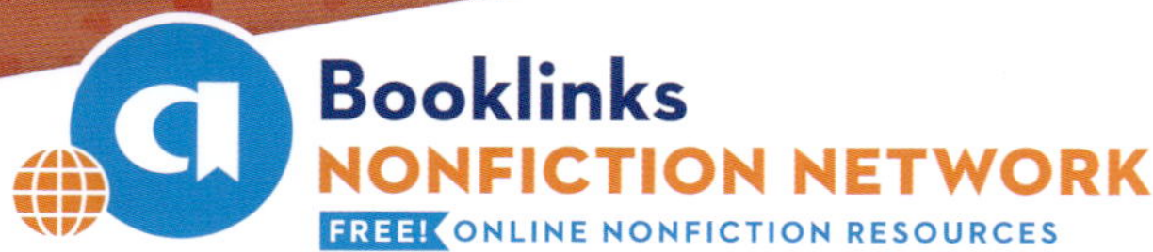

To learn more about the Terracotta Army, please visit **abdobooklinks.com** or scan this QR code. These links are routinely monitored and updated to provide the most current information available.